History of
Hawai'i

La historia de
Hawái

THIS EDITION

Editorial Management by Oriel Square
Produced for DK by WonderLab Group LLC
Jennifer Emmett, Erica Green, Kate Hale, *Founders*

Editor Maya Myers; **Photography Editor** Nicole DiMella; **Managing Editor** Rachel Houghton;
Designers Project Design Company; **Researcher** Michelle Harris;
Copy Editor Lori Merritt; **Indexer** Connie Binder; **Proofreader** Carmen Orozco;
Authenticity Readers Dr. Naomi R. Caldwell, Kale Kanaeholo; **Spanish Translation** Isabel C. Mendoza;
Series Reading Specialist Dr. Jennifer Albro

First American Edition, 2024
Published in the United States by DK Publishing, a division of Penguin Random House LLC
1745 Broadway, 20th Floor, New York, NY 10019

A catalog record for this book is available from the Library of Congress.
HC ISBN: 978-0-7440-9495-4
PB ISBN: 978-0-7440-9494-7

DK books are available at special discounts when purchased in bulk for sales promotions, premiums, fund-raising,
or educational use. For details, contact:
DK Publishing Special Markets, 1745 Broadway, 20th Floor, New York, NY 10019
SpecialSales@dk.com

Printed and bound in China

The publisher would like to thank the following for their kind permission to reproduce their images:
a=above; c=center; b=below; l=left; r=right; t=top; b/g=background
Alamy Stock Photo: Yvette Cardozo 28b, Danita Delimont, Agent / Dave Bartruff 3, Design Pics Inc / Hawaiian
Legacy Archive / Pacific Stock 19t, North Wind Picture Archives 25bl, The Picture Art Collection 18br, Marlon
Trottmann 12br, Chester Voyage 1, Zuma Press, Inc. 10-11, 30clb; **Bishop Museum Archives:** 19cra, 30tl;
Bridgeman Images: Christie's Images 12bl; **Dreamstime.com:** Evan Austen 22-23, Bennymarty 8-9,
Innaastakhova 23crb, Rico Leffanta 16-17, Rainer Lesniewski 8b, Martinmark 4-5, Grondin Franck Olivier 23clb,
Joey Swart 23bc, Juergen Wallstabe 14b, Wirestock 7tr; **Getty Images:** AFP / Mandel Ngan 27tr, Moment / Nisa
and Ulli Maier Photography 6-7, 30bl, Jim Sugar 9br, Universal Images Group Editorial / Pictures from History 21tr;
Getty Images / iStock: Daniel Bendjy 29tr, E+ / Fat Camera 29tl, 30cla, Steven Gaertner 20b;
Hawaii State Archives: 24tl, 25br; **Library of Congress, Washington, D.C.:** LC-DIG-stereo-1s12105 /
Pretty hula dancing girls with wreaths of flowers, Honolulu, Hawaii. Hawaii Honolulu, 1923. Photograph.
https: / / www.loc.gov / item / 2018647440 / . 13t; **The 'Aha'ula Collections:** Brook Kapukuniahi Parker 15t;
The Honolulu Star-Advertiser: John C. Poole 20cr, 30cl

Cover images: *Front:* **Dreamstime.com:** Evgenii Naumov b; **Getty Images:** 500px / Warren Ishii; **Getty Images /
iStock:** Nancy C. Ross r; *Back:* **Alamy Stock Photo:** NZ / BT cra; **Dreamstime.com:** Evgenii Naumov clb

All other images © Dorling Kindersley
For more information see: www.dkimages.com

www.dk.com

This book was made with Forest
Stewardship Council™ certified
paper — one small step in DK's
commitment to a sustainable future.
Learn more at
www.dk.com/uk/information/sustainability

History of Hawai'i

La historia de Hawái

Libby Romero

Contents
Contenido

What Is Hawai´i?
¿Qué es Hawái?

Hawai´i is many things.
It is a chain of islands in the
Pacific Ocean.
It is home to Mauna Loa.
That is the largest active volcano
on Earth.
Big-wave surfing started here.
And Hawai´i is the 50th state in
the USA.

Hawái es muchas cosas.
Es un grupo de islas del
océano Pacífico.
Es el hogar de Mauna Loa.
Ese es el volcán activo más
grande de la Tierra.
Allí también se inició el surf
de olas grandes.
Y Hawái es el estado número
cincuenta de EE. UU.

Mauna Loa

The Hawaiian Islands lie above
a hot spot inside Earth.
The hot spot melts rock.
The melted rock rises to
the surface.

Las islas hawaianas están sobre
un punto caliente del interior de
la Tierra.
El punto caliente derrite la roca.
La roca derretida sube
a la superficie.

It cools and hardens.
It makes islands.

Se enfría y se endurece.
Así se forman las islas.

The First Hawaiians
Los primeros hawaianos

About 1,500 years ago, the first people came to Hawaiʻi.
They came from the Marquesas Islands—about 2,000 miles (3,219 km) away.

Los primeros habitantes de Hawái llegaron hace unos 1500 años. Venían de las islas Marquesas, ubicadas a unas 2000 millas (3219 kilómetros).

The people sailed across the
ocean in big canoes.
They knew how ocean
currents move.
They used the stars to find
their way.

Navegaron por el océano en
grandes canoas.
Sabían cómo se movían las
corrientes del océano.
Usaron las estrellas para guiarse.

Early Hawaiians knew how to farm and fish.
They could carve, weave, and make medicines.
The people honored the land and the sea.
They also honored many gods and goddesses.

Los primeros hawaianos sabían sembrar y pescar.
Sabían tejer y hacer esculturas y medicinas.
Veneraban la tierra y el mar.
También veneraban a varios dioses y diosas.

Kūkāʻilimoku, god of war
Kukailimoku, el dios de la guerra

Pele, goddess of fire and volcanoes
Pele, la diosa del fuego y los volcanes

The people had no
written language.
They sang and chanted stories.
They performed hula, too.
Hula dances told stories.

Este pueblo no tenía un
lenguaje escrito.
Contaban historias con canciones
y cánticos.
También con unas danzas
llamadas hula.

Royal History
Historia de un reino

Over time, more people sailed
to the islands.
The people divided the
land into regions.
They divided themselves
into groups.
Group leaders were called
Ali´i [uh-LEE-ee].

Con el tiempo, otros pueblos
llegaron a las islas.
Se dividió la tierra en regiones.
Los pueblos se dividieron
en grupos.
Los líderes de
los grupos se
llamaban alii.

They were the chiefs.
The chiefs ruled the regions.
But they wanted more power.
They fought to control land.

Ellos eran los caciques.
Los caciques gobernaban las
regiones. Pero querían más
poder. Lucharon por el control
de las tierras.

One chief wanted to unite
the people of the islands.
His name was Kamehameha
[kuh-may-huh-MAY-uh].
Kamehameha battled the
other chiefs.
He won.
In 1810, he became
Hawai´i's first king.

Un cacique quiso unir
a los pueblos de las islas.
Se llamaba Kamehameha.
Kamehameha luchó contra
otros caciques, y ganó.
En 1810, se convirtió en
el primer rey de Hawái.

King Kamehameha I
El rey Kamehameha I

Kamehameha ruled for nine years.
After he died, his oldest son
became king.
Kamehameha II helped make
a written language for his people.
When he died, his younger
brother ruled.
Under Kamehameha III,Hawaiians
learned to read their language.

Kamehameha reinó durante
nueve años.
Después de su muerte, su hijo
mayor se convirtió en el rey.
Kamehameha II ayudó a crear un
lenguaje escrito para su pueblo.
Cuando murió, su hermano
menor subió al trono.
Durante el reinado de
Kamehameha III, los
hawaianos aprendieron
a leer su idioma.

King Kamehameha III
El rey Kamehameha III

constitution
constitución

In 1840, Kamehameha III
announced a new constitution.
He shared his power with
the people.
Hawai´i became an
independent kingdom.

En 1840, Kamehameha III creó
una nueva constitución.
Compartió su poder con el pueblo.
Hawái se convirtió en un
reino independiente.

Time of Change
Tiempos de cambio

People from other places heard
about Hawai´i.
They saw opportunity.
So, people flocked to live
on the islands.
And Hawai´i began to change.

En otros lugares, se comenzó
a hablar de Hawái.
Mucha gente vio oportunidades.
Por eso, montones de inmigrantes
llegaron a las islas.
Y Hawái comenzó
a cambiar.

Captain James Cook was the first European to set foot on the islands. He sailed there in 1778.
In 1820, American missionaries arrived. They built churches. They preached against Native Hawaiian beliefs and traditions. Hawaiian culture began to fade away.

El capitán James Cook fue el primer europeo que llegó a las islas. Navegó hasta allí en 1778.
En 1820, llegaron misioneros estadounidenses que construyeron iglesias. Predicaron en contra de las creencias y tradiciones de los indígenas hawaianos. La cultura hawaiana comenzó a perderse.

Captain James Cook
El capitán James Cook

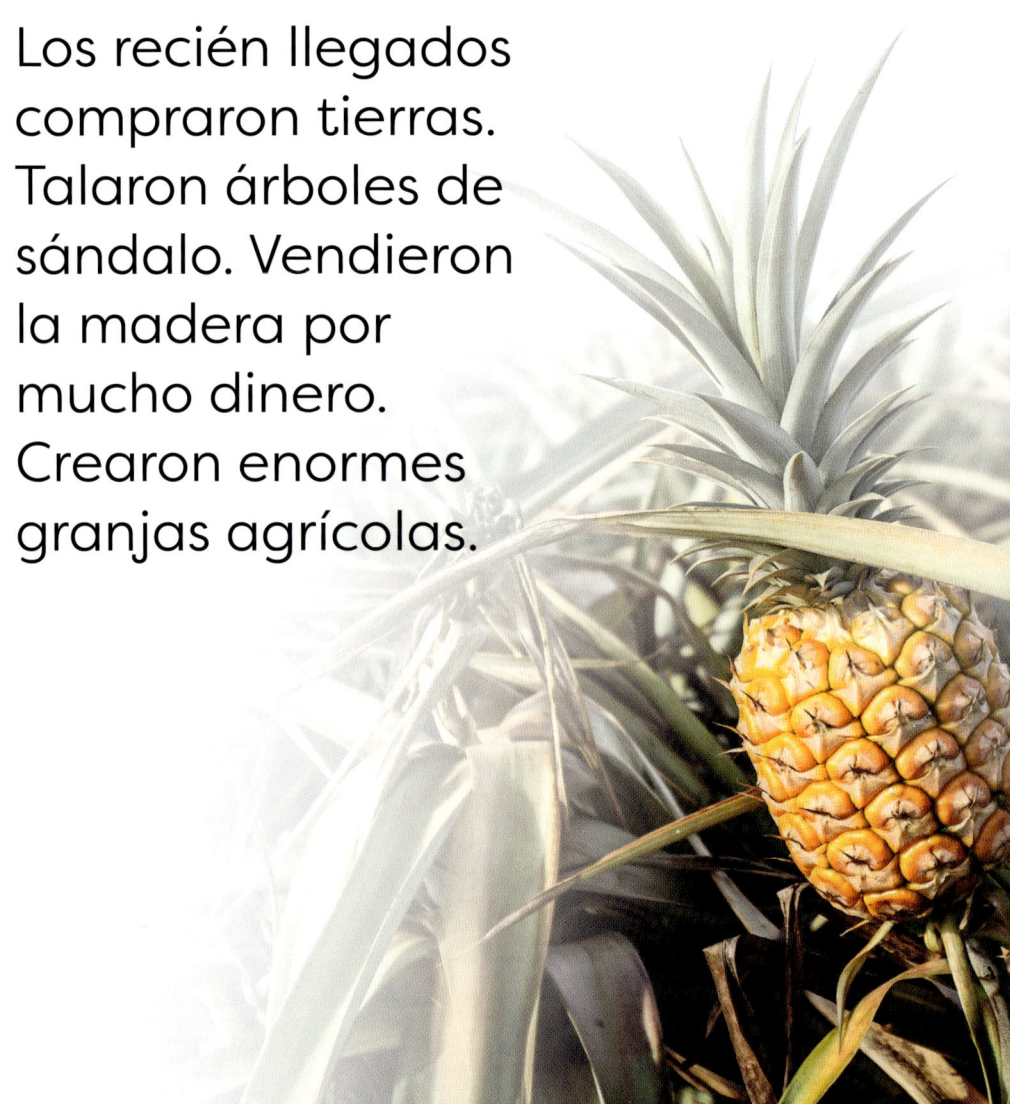

Newcomers bought land.
They cut down sandalwood trees.
They sold the wood for a lot
of money.
They planted large farms.

Los recién llegados
compraron tierras.
Talaron árboles de
sándalo. Vendieron
la madera por
mucho dinero.
Crearon enormes
granjas agrícolas.

They grew sugarcane, coffee,
and pineapple.
Workers came from all over
the world.
Soon, there were more newcomers
than Native Hawaiians on
the islands.

Cultivaron caña de azúcar,
café y piña.
De todas partes del mundo
llegaron trabajadores.
En poco tiempo, ya había en las
islas más extranjeros que
indígenas hawaianos.

King Kalākaua
El rey Kalakaua

In 1887, wealthy landowners forced King Kalākaua [kah-LAH-kao-ah] to sign a new constitution. It took power away from Native Hawaiians. It gave power to foreign landowners. Lili´uokalani [lee-LEE-ooh-oh-kah-lah-nee] was Hawai´i's last queen.

En 1887, terratenientes ricos obligaron al rey Kalakaua a aprobar una nueva constitución. Esta les quitó poder a los indígenas hawaianos. Les dio poder a los terratenientes extranjeros. Liliuokalani fue la última reina de Hawái.

She tried to give power back
to the people.
But rich Americans took over
the government.
In 1900, Hawai´i became
a US territory.
In 1959, it became a US state.

Ella trató de regresarle el poder
al pueblo.
Pero los estadounidenses ricos
se apoderaron del gobierno.
En 1900, Hawái se convirtió
en un territorio de EE. UU.
En 1959, se convirtió
en un estado de EE. UU.

Queen Lili´uokalani
La reina Liliuokalani

Hawai´i Today
Hawái hoy

Today, millions of people visit
Hawai´i each year.
Visitors go to ´Iolani Palace.
That is where Hawai´i's kings
and queens lived.
Visitors tour the capital, Honolulu.

Hoy, millones de personas visitan
Hawái cada año.
Los turistas van
al Palacio Lolani.
Allí vivieron los reyes
y las reinas de Hawái.
Los turistas recorren
la capital, Honolulu.

Barack Obama
was born there.
He was the 44th
president of the USA.

Allí nació
Barack Obama.
Obama fue el
presidente número
cuarenta y cuatro de EE. UU.

Barack Obama

Only one in 10 people living
in Hawai´i today is a
Native Hawaiian.
But the Hawaiian culture is strong.
Children learn from their parents.
They surf along Hawai´i's shores.

Hoy, solo uno de cada diez
habitantes de Hawái es
indígena hawaiano.
Pero la cultura
hawaiana es fuerte.
Los niños aprenden
mucho de sus padres.
Surfean en las
costas de Hawái.

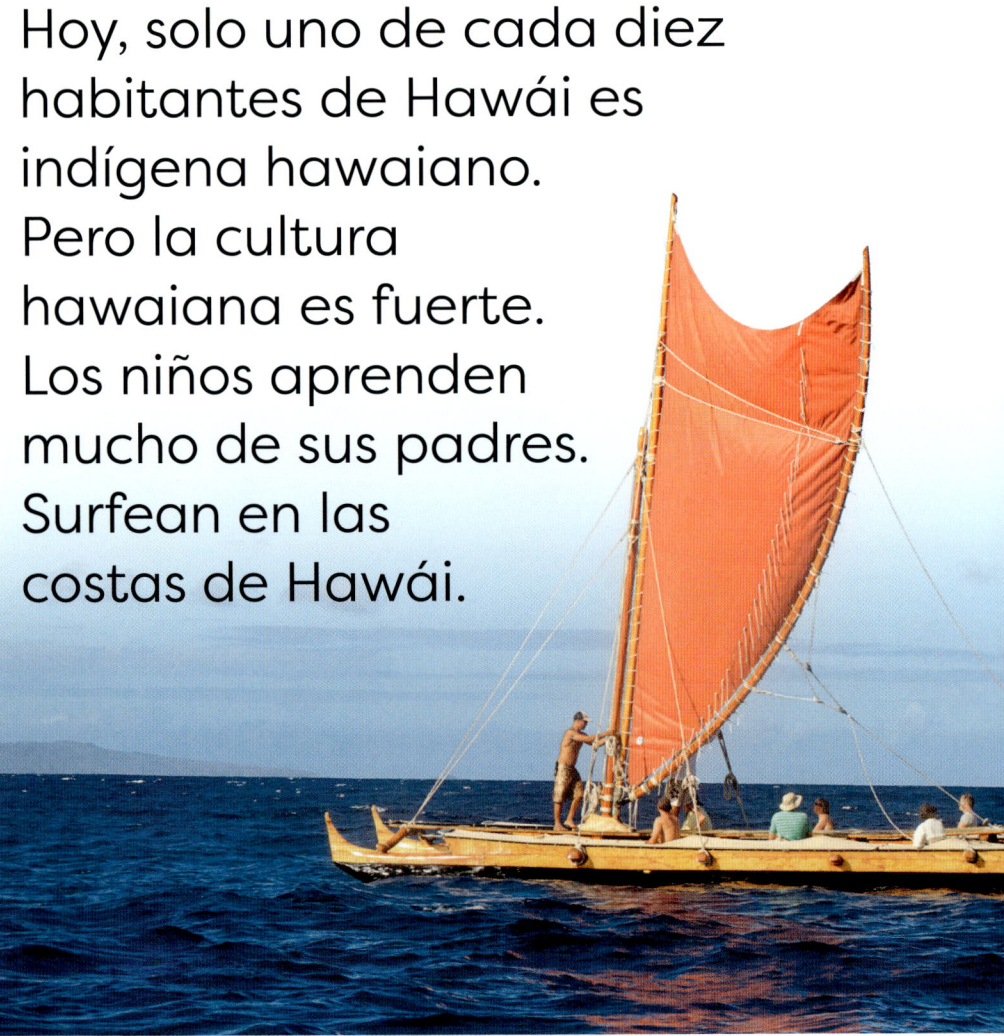

They build
canoes and perform hula.
Native Hawaiians celebrate
traditions that started here
long ago.
They share their culture with
the world.

Construyen canoas y bailan hula.
Los indígenas hawaianos celebran
tradiciones que comenzaron allí
hace mucho tiempo.
Comparten su cultura con
el mundo.

Glossary
Glosario

constitution
a document containing the laws used to govern a nation

constitución
un documento que contiene las normas para gobernar una nación

current
the movement of a body of water in a certain direction

corriente
el movimiento de un cuerpo de agua en cierta dirección

hula
a traditional Hawaiian dance

hula
una danza tradicional hawaiana

missionaries
people sent by a church to teach or convert others to their religion

misioneros
gente enviada por una iglesia para enseñar a otros su religión, o convertirlos

surfing
riding the ocean waves on a surfboard

surfear
deslizarse sobre las olas del océano usando una tabla

Index
Índice

Quiz
Prueba

Answer the questions to see what you have learned. Check your answers with an adult.

1. How did ancient people first get to Hawai´i?
2. Which chief united the Hawaiian Islands?
3. Who was the first European to visit Hawai´i?
4. How did missionaries work to change Hawai´i?
5. Which US president was born in Hawai´i?

1. They sailed across the ocean in big canoes 2. Kamehameha I
3. Captain James Cook 4. They built churches and preached against Native Hawaiian beliefs and traditions 5. Barack Obama

Responde las preguntas para saber cuánto aprendiste. Verifica tus respuestas con un adulto.

1. ¿Cómo llegaron a Hawái sus primeros habitantes?
2. ¿Qué cacique unió los pueblos de las islas de Hawái?
3. ¿Quién fue el primer europeo que llegó a Hawái?
4. ¿Qué hicieron los misioneros para cambiar Hawái?
5. ¿Qué presidente de EE. UU. nació en Hawái?

1. Navegaron por el océano en grandes canoas. 2. Kamehameha I 3. El capitán James Cook 4. Construyeron iglesias y predicaron en contra de las creencias y tradiciones de los indígenas hawaianos. 5. Barack Obama